Managing Bank Accounts and Investments

Xina M. Uhl and Jeri Freedman

Rosen
YA™
New York

Published in 2020 by The Rosen Publishing Group, Inc.
29 East 21st Street, New York, NY 10010

Library of Congress Cataloging-in-Publication Data

Names: Uhl, Xina M., author. | Freedman, Jeri, author.
Title: Managing bank accounts and investments / Xina M. Uhl and
Jeri Freedman.
Description: First edition. | New York : Rosen Publishing,
[2020] | Series: Managing your money and finances | Includes
bibliographical references and index.
Identifiers: LCCN 2018048188| ISBN 9781508188490 (library
bound) | ISBN 9781508188483 (pbk.)
Subjects: LCSH: Bank accounts—Juvenile literature. | Investments—
Juvenile literature. | Finance, Personal—Juvenile literature.
Classification: LCC HG1660.A3 U39 2020 | DDC 332.6—dc23
LC record available at https://lccn.loc.gov/2018048188

Manufactured in the United States of America

CONTENTS

INTRODUCTION

Money makes the world go 'round. It may be a cliché, but it is a true one. One of the most important things you will have to do as a young adult is to learn how to properly handle your finances. By establishing good habits while you are young, you will ensure that you have a life that is free from unnecessary problems with debt and budgeting. Your money can work for you if you make wise investments. By setting up a habit of saving your money, it will increase over time. It is necessary to prepare for retirement while you are young, even though it is many years in the future. If you wait to save money for retirement, you will have lost out on many years of interest earnings. In fact, saving for retirement while you are young can earn you twice as much money as you might have if you had started later. The interest that you earn will be added to your balance. That means that the entire amount will, in turn, earn more interest. Over a long period of time, the funds will grow at an impressive rate.

While it can be tempting to spend every dime you make, it is a big mistake. A portion of money that you earn should always be set aside for later. In order to do this, you will need to learn how to budget, or plan out how much money you receive and how much you can spend. By establishing a budget, you will always know how much money you have—and don't have. Finances do not need to be stressful, as they are for many people, if you stick to a budget.

Your first impulse upon getting a job may be to spend everything you make. But that is an unwise decision that can affect your life for decades into the future.

On May 18, 2018, in an article by Anna Bahney, CNN reported the grim facts about Americans and money. Four out of ten Americans do not have savings to cover a $400 unexpected expense. To come up with the money, these Americans would have to borrow it or sell something. Selling your possessions is not fun, and you are likely to get only a portion of the money you paid for them to begin with. Borrowing money comes with a cost: interest that is due on top of the amount borrowed. Sometimes this interest rate can be high. Another 25 percent of Americans are in worse shape. They have saved no money at all for retirement. A life of poverty and lack of basic needs, like health care, being met can result from having no retirement savings. It is a serious situation that you would do well to avoid. Many people dream of having a retirement filled with travel and enjoyment of friends and family. These activities are much more enjoyable than living a life of lack.

The good news is that saving and investments can pay off if you learn how to approach them wisely. This guide explains bank accounts, budgeting, interest, money markets, stocks, bonds, types of retirement accounts, and more. The world of finances and investments can seem overwhelming. By learning about each category of accounts, stocks, and bonds, you can dip your toe into a world that can help all your financial dreams come true.

CHAPTER **ONE**

All About Bank Accounts

Bank accounts come in a number of types, depending on your needs and your financial situation. By learning about each of them, you can decide which is appropriate for you.

The purpose of a checking account is to keep your money in a safe place—the bank—while you use it to pay for short-term expenses. You can take money out of a checking account by writing a check or using an ATM (automated teller machine) card (also called a check or debit card), as described later in this chapter.

The purpose of a savings account is to put money away for long-term needs. To encourage you to put money into the bank and leave it there, the bank will pay you interest. Interest is an amount of money equal to some percentage of the money in your account. For example, a bank may pay 3 percent interest annually (each year) on money in a savings account. If you put $1,000 in this bank, you would earn $30 in interest at the end of one year.

The computer revolution has provided you with a number of tools to easily manage your bank accounts and investments.

Some banks offer interest-paying checking accounts. You can write checks on these accounts, too, but the bank pays a small amount of interest on the amount (balance) you leave in the bank. The interest rate on interest-paying checking accounts is usually lower than that paid on savings accounts. In addition, you may be required to keep a certain amount of money (a minimum balance) in an interest-paying checking account.

Many banks offer a type of investment called a certificate of deposit (CD). When you buy a CD, you agree to invest your money with the bank for a specific period of time. The bank, in turn, agrees to pay you a specific rate of interest on the money you invest. CDs come in a variety of durations (lengths of time) and minimum amounts. For example, you can buy a CD that lasts for six months, one year, or longer. Usually, the longer the

Current Investment Offerings

	Minimum Balance	Interest Rate%	Annual Percentage Yield (APY)%
Certificates of Deposit			
30 days	$500	0.05%	0.05%
90 days	$500	0.20%	0.20%
6 months	$500	0.30%	0.30%
12 months	$500	0.45%	0.45%
18 months	$500	0.50%	0.50%
24 months	$500	0.55%	0.55%
36 months	$500	0.65%	0.65%
48 months	$500	0.75%	0.75%
60 months	$500	1.00%	1.00%
Individual Retirement Account			
Small Saver IRA		0.40%	0.40%
Checking and Savings Accounts			
Your Choice Checking		0.10%	0.10%
Interest Checking	$500	0.20%	0.20%
Money Market $0–$2,499	$500	0.65%	0.65%
Statement Savings			

Mortga

Fixed R

Investing for retirement when you are young works: $10,000 invested at age twenty earning 5 percent annual interest will be almost $100,000 at age sixty-five.

duration of the CD and the larger the minimum amount you are required to invest, the higher the interest. CDs provide a higher return on investment (or profit) than savings accounts and interest-paying checking accounts. However, there is usually a penalty fee that you must pay if you take your money out before you are supposed to.

About Interest

Interest is money the bank pays you for the use of your money. There are two types of interest: simple and compound. Simple interest is a flat percentage calculated on a sum of money, called the principal. The money you place in an account or receive as a

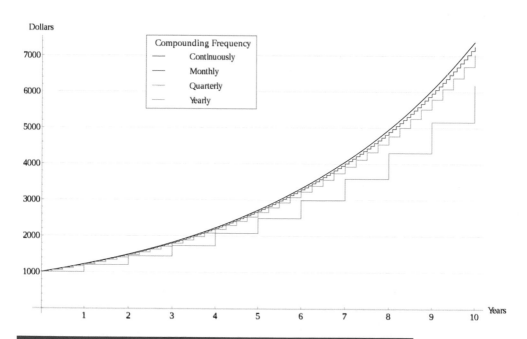

This chart demonstrates the upward pattern of compounded interest. While it takes years to become a significant amount of money, such waiting will profit you in the long run.

loan is the principal. If you put $1,000 in a bank account, that $1,000 is your principal.

Simple interest is calculated as follows:

Principal × Interest Rate (with the percent converted to decimal format) = Interest

In this example, where the interest rate is 10 percent, the interest would be:

$1,000 × .10 = $100

You will not often encounter simple interest in banking and investment transactions, however. In most cases, you will be dealing with compound interest. Compound interest is calculated on the principal, plus any interest already received. Thus, every month, the amount of your principal will go up, and the amount of interest you receive will be larger. The point to remember is that compound interest is a very effective way to grow a small amount of money into a much larger sum of money. Every month, the amount on which the interest is based increases. You can find out how much money you will earn from compound interest in a given period of time by using the following formula:

V = P(1 + R/F)FY

Where:

V = Total value
P = Initial principal
R = Interest rate

F = Frequency (number of times per year interest is calculated)

Y = Number of years

Let's return to our example of $1,000 with an interest rate of 10 percent per year. Compounded monthly (twelve months per year) over a period of five years, this would be:

$V = \$1,000(1 + .10/12)12 \times 5 =$
$V = \$1,000(1 + .0083)60 =$
$V = \$1,000 \times 1.008360 =$
$V = \$1,000 \times 1.64 =$
$\$1,640$

Thus, at the end of five years, you will have earned $1,640. Note that 1.64 is 1.0083 multiplied by itself 60 times. But don't despair—there are many online compound interest calculators that will calculate the interest for you. One online example is www.webmath.com/compinterest.html, or simply go to www .google.com and search for "compound interest calculator."

Protections for Your Money in the Bank

Banks make most of their money from the interest they get on loans they make to people and businesses. Where do they get the money they lend? From people who put money into accounts with the bank. You put money in the bank, and the bank lends that money to other people.

You might worry that if the bank lends people money and they don't pay it back, the bank won't have the money to give you when you try to take your money back out (withdraw it). However, the Federal Deposit Insurance Corporation (FDIC), an agency of the US government, insures any money up to $250,000 that you put in a US bank account. Furthermore, this insurance applies to each bank you deposit money in. So, if you had $250,000 in Bank 1 and $250,000 in Bank 2, your money in both banks would be protected. Be aware that FDIC insurance applies only to money placed in checking accounts, savings accounts, money markets, and CDs. Some banks offer investment accounts, such as mutual funds (which are discussed in chapter 4). Money in stock and bond mutual funds is not protected by FDIC insurance. However, reputable brokerage firms carry insurance provided by the Securities Investment Protection Corporation, which protects your investments up to $500,000 if the brokerage firm fails.

The FDIC sticker in the window of your bank or credit union assures you that the money in your personal accounts is protected by the government.

Check Writing

When you open a checking account, the bank will provide you with checks. The diagram on page TK shows the main parts of a check. It will come printed with your name and address, the name of the bank, and an identifying number indicating which bank the check comes from. At the bottom of the check are two long numbers. The first is a routing number, which identifies the bank that the check comes from. The second number is your

Understanding How to Read a Personal Check

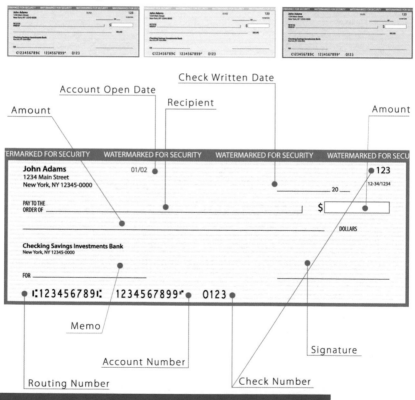

When filling in the amounts in numbers and words on the check, start as close to the edge of the line as possible so that no one can add numbers to the amounts.

account number. These numbers are read by automated systems used by banks for electronically transferring funds. Though checks are not used as much today as in the past, they are still routinely issued for large expenses.

Making Deposits

Of course, before you can take money out of a bank account, you have to put it in. Putting money into a bank is called making a deposit. If you are depositing a check, for example from a part-time or summer job, you will need to do two things. You must endorse the check and then fill out a deposit slip. If you are depositing cash, you will just need to fill out a deposit slip.

   To endorse a check, you simply need to sign your name on the back. It is also a good idea to write your account number on the back of the check. (This is especially true if you are depositing the check through an ATM or through a mobile app.) You can then hand the check or cash and the deposit slip to a teller, deposit it in an ATM, or use a mobile banking app to deposit it. Deposit slips are usually provided in the back of each book of checks. They are also available at the bank.

   List the amount of each check in the space provided and total them. The line to the left of the check amount is for the identifying number of the bank from which each check comes. This helps the bank's staff identify which deposit a check belongs to, if it becomes separated from the deposit slip. Some people omit this number and just list the amount. If you do this, it's a good idea to write your account number on the back of the check. If you are using a blank deposit slip supplied by the bank instead of a preprinted one, be sure to fill in your name, address, phone number, and account number. If you have more checks than there are spaces on the front of the deposit slip, you can list them in additional spaces provided on the back of the deposit slip. You then total the additional checks and write the total in the space provided on the front of the deposit slip.

Debit Cards

In addition to checks, banks today provide account holders with an ATM card (also called a check card or debit card) that they can use to access the money in their accounts. When you get an ATM card, you choose a code consisting of several numbers. This is your personal identification number, or PIN. Because anyone who finds out your account number and PIN can take money out of your accounts, never tell anyone your PIN number. And be sure to pick one that's easy for you to remember. You should never write your PIN down and carry it in your purse or wallet or leave it in your desk where someone can find it.

To use an ATM card, you insert it into a slot on an auto-mated teller machine and type in your PIN. You will then see a menu that allows you to perform activities like withdrawing money, depositing money, or getting the balance in your ac-count. The balance is the amount of money currently available in your account.

Many stores and restaurants also accept ATM cards as a form of payment. In some cases, you will run the ATM card through a card reader and enter your PIN. In other cases, a cashier will process the transaction the same way that he or she would process a credit card. Either way, the money for the purchase is immediately deducted (subtracted) from your bank account.

Paying on the Go

Gaining in popularity are online and mobile payment apps, such as PayPal, Zelle, and Venmo. These apps can be used to pay bills or send money to people. First, users must sign up for an account and link that account to their checking account, debit card, or credit card. PayPal, Zelle, and Venmo require the email address or mobile phone number of the person to be paid. The advantage of using these apps is that they transfer money quickly and easily. They also provide another line of defense against thieves trying to access your bank accounts or credit cards. Of course, you should also be careful to safeguard your login and username for these apps or you might find yourself a victim of online fraud.

The Right Bank for You

There are two main factors to consider when choosing a bank: cost and convenience. Most banks charge a fee for using their services. The fee may be a flat monthly charge, such as $8 per month. Or, it may be a per unit fee, such as $.50 for every withdrawal from a savings account. Every bank has a listing of the various types of checking and savings accounts it offers and the fees associated with each. In many cases, there is no fee if you keep a certain minimum balance in the account at all times, such as $1,000 or $2,500.

Before you open a bank account, you should make the rounds of your local banks and obtain a list of the fees and minimum

Many banks offer special bonuses when you set up an account with them. These bonuses can be significant.

balances for various types of accounts. You can then see which bank has the lowest fees for the amount of money you'll likely be depositing.

First, you must be able to get to the bank easily. So, you will most likely want to choose a bank close to where you live, go to school, or work—or, better yet, one with branches close to all of these places. Second, you may want to choose a bank with conveniently located ATMs so that you can easily access your accounts. You can probably use your ATM card at other banks' ATMs. However, most banks charge a fee ranging from $1 to several dollars if you use an ATM card that doesn't come from that bank.

To open a bank account, you will need to bring to the bank the money for the initial deposit, a photo ID (such as a passport or driver's license), and a Social Security card. If you do not have a passport or driver's license, you can obtain a state-issued photo ID by bringing your birth certificate to your state registry of motor vehicles. A bank representative will then set up the account for you. You must be eighteen years old to open a bank account; if you are younger, your parent or guardian will have to open it for you.

Credit unions are an alternative to banks that offer many advantages. Credit unions are made of an organized group of people, such as those from a particular area, company, or association. They pool their money together and offer low-cost loans to members. Credit unions function in almost exactly the same way that banks do but they are more limited to local areas. Typically, monthly fees are absent or less expensive than many banks.

Now that you know how to choose your bank and open your accounts, the next chapter will provide you with information on managing your bank accounts.

CHAPTER TWO

Keeping Track of Your Bank Account

Unless you keep track of each amount you put into and take out of your bank accounts, you can quickly run into trouble. Just missing a few transactions—or one if it is big enough—can result in bouncing a check, or having the bank reject the check you have written. That means that the vendor you wrote the check to will not be paid until you put enough money in your account. It also means that the bank will charge you a hefty overdraft fee.

Why You Must Reconcile Your Checking Account

Each box of checks that you buy comes with a special notebook called a check register. Every time you write a check or make a deposit, you should note it in the check register.

At the end of each month, you will receive a statement from your bank. A statement is a list of every deposit and withdrawal

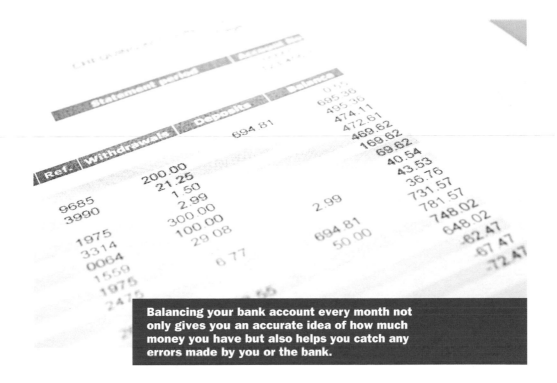

Balancing your bank account every month not only gives you an accurate idea of how much money you have but also helps you catch any errors made by you or the bank.

you made, every check that the bank paid, and any interest the bank has paid you. Your bank should have an option to download your statement online. You can also export the statement information to a spreadsheet, or program such as Quicken or Acemoney if you prefer. You can use the statement to verify exactly how much money you have in each account. The verification process is called reconciling, or balancing, your checkbook. Since it's easy to forget to enter a check in your register, balancing your checkbook is an important way to keep from bouncing checks.

To balance your checkbook, first compare each check, withdrawal, debit card purchase, and deposit listed on the statement with what you have listed in your register. You should check off each item in the register. What you are left with will be checks you have written that the bank has not yet received (outstanding checks). You may also have deposits that you made after the statement was mailed to you. Subtract any outstanding checks from the ending balance total on the statement. Add any additional deposits. This will give you an accurate total of how much money you actually have in your account. Update this number in your check register if necessary.

Online Account Access

Most banks today allow you to manage your account over the

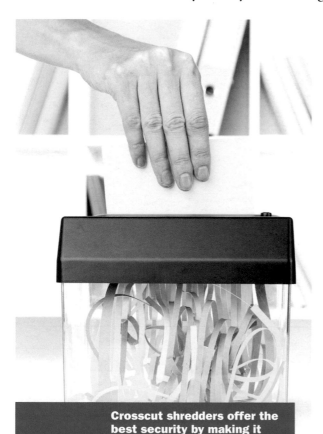

Crosscut shredders offer the best security by making it impossible to reassemble the strips of paper.

internet. To do so, go to your bank's website and look for an area on the home page that says something like "Online Banking." There should be a link there that says "Enroll" or "Register." When you click that link, you will be asked to provide information like your account number and a username and password. Once you have enrolled, you will be able to log in with your username and password. There are many functions you can perform online, such as checking the transactions that have taken place in

Identity Theft Is Everywhere

Identity theft is a fast-growing crime. It is very important that you protect your username, password, PIN, and account numbers for all your investment and bank accounts. Never write down any of this information on paper or sticky notes. Do not use easily guessable numbers, such as the last four digits of your phone number, your birthday, or the name of your dog, as a password. When you get paper statements for your accounts, bills, and offers for new credit cards, do not throw these in the trash or recycling. Instead, get a small shredder and shred them before throwing them out. Most banks and investment firms offer an "email-only" option for statements. If you have regular online access, you may choose to use this option.

your account. You can see the deposits, withdrawals, and interest payments. You may also be able to transfer money from one of your accounts to another, update your address information, get copies of statements, make payments for credit cards or loans you have with the bank, stop payment on a check, and order checks. In some cases, banks offer additional online tools like a checkbook balancer, which you can use to reconcile your checkbook. In addition, some banks offer similar mobile banking services, which people can use with a smartphone or tablet.

Guard your password carefully since it is the key to your private information. Hackers are always trying new ways to steal money from unwary individuals.

Do not keep passwords, PINs, or account numbers on your computer. Computers are easy to steal, and hackers are always trying to find new ways to read the data on your computer's hard drive. Do not leave your browser open with any bank or investment-related screens open. Casual passers-by can easily gain access to your accounts if you do. Most browsers—including those on smartphones—allow users to back up page by page. For this reason, you should always close the browser completely when you've been viewing one of your accounts, especially on smartphones and tablets, which are easily lost.

In addition to online tools provided by banks, there are also a number of software programs that you can purchase to manage your finances. The best-known software for this purpose

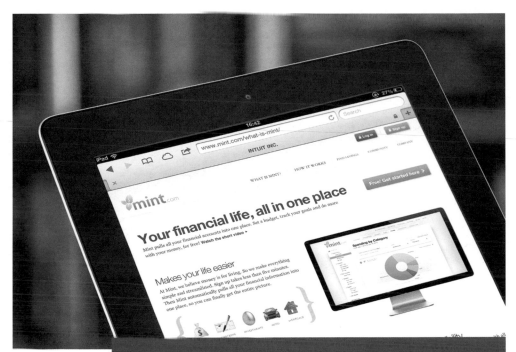

Mint is one of a number of free personal finance apps that can help you budget and establish financial goals.

is Quicken. Such software provides you with an online check register, but it goes further than that. It provides the ability to keep track of your investments. It automatically downloads information from your bank and investment account. In addition, it provides you with the ability to create a variety of reports, including budgets, reports that show you what you've spent your money on, and reports that tell you how your investments are doing.

Mint or YNAB are popular online personal finance applications that you may want to use to manage your accounts. These apps make it easy to keep track of your expenses, make financial goals, and manage the income and expenses in your accounts. Mint is free to use, while YNAB charges a fee.

CHAPTER THREE

Looking Ahead to the Future

Making investments is an essential activity to undertake for two reasons: retirement and increasing your wealth. Although it can be tempting to put off saving for retirement while you are young, you are losing out on an opportunity to increase your money since it grows fastest if you start investing early in your working life. Making smart investments also means that you can grow what you manage to save.

It's Not Too Soon to Start

One of the most important things you can do financially is invest for retirement. You might think, "I'm very young. Why should I worry about retirement when I get my first job? I can do that when I get older." The answer is that, as with savings accounts, the longer your money is making a profit, the more you get from

Spending time with grandparents can provide you with more than good memories. It can also remind you that one day you, too, will need adequate money for your retirement.

compounding. There are two main types of accounts used for retirement investing: 401(k) plans and individual retirement accounts (IRAs).

A Popular Plan

The 401(k) plan takes its name from the section of the tax code that describes it. A company sets up a 401(k) plan for its employees. Employees can contribute up to a certain percentage of their salary, for example, 15 percent. In most cases, the company will match, dollar for dollar, some amount of the money that the employee contributes, for example, 3 percent. The company typically offers a variety of stock, bond, and money market funds in which employees can invest. The money put into

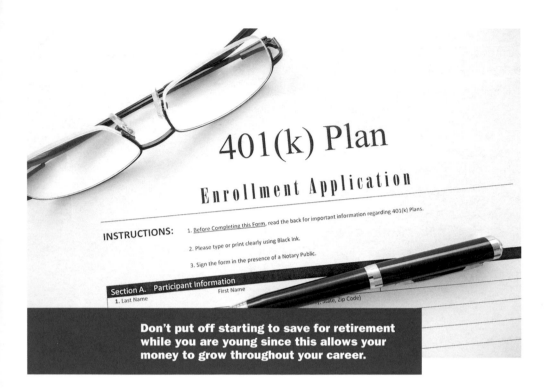

Don't put off starting to save for retirement while you are young since this allows your money to grow throughout your career.

401(k) plans is pretax dollars, which means that the amount you invest is subtracted from your income for tax purposes. You pay taxes on the money when you withdraw it. If you remove money from a 401(k) account before you are fifty-five years old, you must pay a 10 percent penalty in addition to taxes.

Individual Retirement Accounts

Unlike a 401(k) plan, which is established by a company, an IRA is established by an individual. Even people who have a 401(k) plan can have an IRA. At the time of this writing, the amount you can contribute to an IRA per year is $5,500 ($6,500 for people who are fifty or older). The amount you are allowed to contribute is adjusted annually. There are two types of IRAs:

traditional IRAs and Roth IRAs. In a traditional IRA, the money you contribute is subtracted from your earnings before you pay taxes. Thus, the payment of taxes on that part of your income is put off, or deferred, until you withdraw the money in your IRA. This type of IRA is best for people who expect to earn less money when they retire than they will while they're working because their tax rate will be lower once they retire.

The second type of IRA is called a Roth IRA because the bill that created it was introduced into the US Senate by Senator William V. Roth of Delaware. When you invest in a Roth IRA, you use money on which you have already paid taxes. However, any money you earn in the Roth IRA is nontaxable. That means you will not have to pay taxes on it when you take it out.

Starting your own business can provide freedom and financial success if you meet the needs of the market and manage your finances carefully.

This type of IRA is best for people who expect to have the same or greater earnings when they reach retirement age.

Growing Your Wealth

There is a second reason for investing—financial security. Having money gives you the ability to realize many of your dreams: owning a house, starting a business, working for yourself, and other ambitions. Many people struggle to accomplish their desires on the money they earn at their jobs. The answer is to put a little money away on a regular basis. This way you can build up savings that you can use one day to do the things you want.

Learning About Investments

Today, there are at least three major cable TV channels devoted to information on financial and investment subjects: CNBC, Fox Business News, and Bloomberg TV. There are several magazines and newspapers devoted to investment news. Among the most reputable are the newspapers the *Wall Street Journal*, *Barron's*, and *Investor's Business Daily*, and magazines like *Smart Money*, *Money*, and *Kiplinger's*, which have helpful articles on managing your money as well as investing.

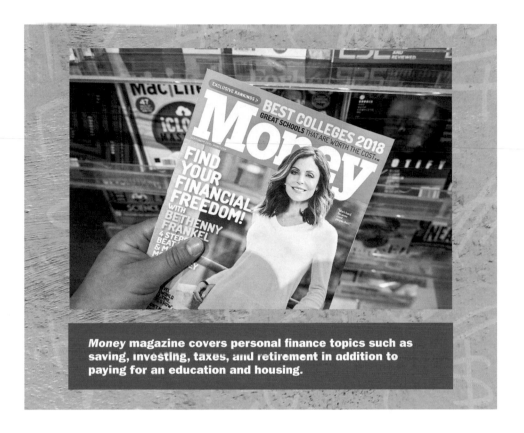

Money magazine covers personal finance topics such as saving, investing, taxes, and retirement in addition to paying for an education and housing.

Are the Risks Worth the Reward?

At the heart of investing is the concept of risk. You invest because you think you can make money. However, there is also the risk that you can lose the money you invest. For example, you could buy a share of stock for $10, and it could increase in value to $50 or decrease in value to $0. Some stocks are riskier than others. Often, the riskier an investment is, the greater its potential gain. However, a larger potential gain can also mean a larger potential loss. How much risk is appropriate depends primarily on the following three factors:

One day you may decide to get married and have children. By looking ahead to your goals, you can plan what type of investments you need to make them come to pass.

Your age: The younger you are, the longer you have to gain back money you lose because you most likely have many working—and investing—years ahead of you.

Your financial situation: If you are supporting a family or saving for graduate school, then you may want to take on less risk with your money than when you did not have those responsibilities. As a general rule, money you are going to need in the next few years for a specific goal, such as paying for college or buying a house, should be kept in very safe forms of investments like CDs.

Your personality: Some people are very adventurous. Others get nervous when they feel the money they've earned is at risk. Different people are comfortable with different amounts of risk.

CHAPTER FOUR

Investing Basics

J ust like bank accounts, investments come in different forms depending on your goals and what you have available to work with. Money markets, bonds, and stocks are the most popular categories.

A Supercharged Savings Account

A money market account is a special type of savings account offered by some banks and investment firms. Money market accounts work in the same way as regular checking or savings accounts, but instead of lending the money from deposits, the bank uses the money to buy and sell different currencies around the world. The interest paid on money market accounts is usually higher than that paid on regular checking accounts.

Types of Bonds

You can purchase US savings bonds online from the US Department of the Treasury for as little as $25.

Bonds basically represent a loan to a company or government. When a company (including banks and public utilities) or government needs to raise money, it often issues bonds. When you buy a bond, you are paid interest at regular intervals, such as monthly, quarterly (four times a year), or annually. There are several different types of bonds, including the following:

Treasury bonds: These are bonds issued by the federal government; they are available in two-, five-, and ten-year periods. These periods refer to the bonds' maturity dates (when the loan must be paid back to you).

Municipal bonds: Municipal bonds are issued by governments other than the federal government, such as states or cities. The interest earned on many municipal bonds is not taxed as long as you live in the state where the bond is issued.

Corporate bonds: Corporate bonds are issued by companies. The interest rate on corporate bonds often varies with how financially sound the company issuing them is. Riskier companies often pay higher interest rates than very sound companies in order to get people to buy their bonds.

How do you know how risky a bond is? There are companies that specialize in rating bonds. Examples of such companies are Moody's Investors Service and Standard & Poor's. They evaluate each company's financial state and give its bonds a rating. For example, Standard & Poor's rates bonds from AAA to D, with AAA being the most sound. Bonds with very low ratings are sometimes called junk bonds. They pay a high rate of interest but are risky because the company that issues them may fail.

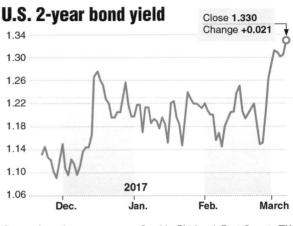

U.S. 2-year bond yield

Close **1.330**
Change **+0.021**

1.34
1.30
1.26
1.22
1.18
1.14
1.10
1.06

2017

Dec.   Jan.   Feb.   March

Source: investing.com   Graphic: Pittsburgh Post-Gazette/TNS

By charting an investment's overall rises and falls, you can understand how the market goes up and down.

Stock Funds

Mutual funds are a type of investment in which many people pool their money to buy an assortment of stocks. By investing in a mutual fund, you get to invest in a variety of companies without having to buy shares of each one individually. Buying shares in a mutual fund can allow you to buy shares in companies you couldn't afford to buy alone. Mutual funds are offered by a large number of investment firms, such as Fidelity Investments, Vanguard, and T. Rowe Price. A mutual fund is managed by a professional who works for the company offering the mutual fund. He or she picks the stocks that the mutual fund contains and decides when to buy more or sell them. Individuals buy shares in the mutual fund in the same way they would buy shares of stock. There are many different types of mutual funds, some specializing in particular countries or industries. For a beginning investor, however, often the best choice is a diversified mutual fund, which invests in a wide range of companies in major industries. Such funds will be discussed later in this chapter.

There are two basic types of mutual funds: load and no load. "Load" refers to the percentage of the invested amount that the mutual fund company keeps as a fee when you buy shares. When the company does not charge for investing in the fund, it is said to be a no-load fund. There are many large mutual fund companies that offer no-load funds. In general, unless you are investing in a special type of fund that gives you limited choices, it is preferable to purchase no-load funds. Mutual fund companies provide a booklet called a prospectus for each fund they offer. This booklet explains the investment strategy of the fund, the companies it invests in, its past performance, factors that could affect the fund, and the fees it charges. You should read the prospectus carefully before investing.

Understanding Your Fund's Performance

How well is your mutual fund doing? You can find out by comparing it to an index. An index is a standard measure of the performance of the stock market as a whole. It is based on the stocks of companies on major stock markets. For example, Dow Jones & Company tracks the performance of thirty major American industrial companies and provides an average of their performance, known as the Dow Jones Industrial Average. By comparing the performance of a mutual fund to an appropriate index, you can see if the fund is performing as well as the stock market in general.

The All-Important Stock Market

A share of stock essentially represents a tiny portion of a company's profits. Stocks are sold in various stock markets. There are a number of different stock markets (also called stock exchanges). The two major ones are the New York Stock Exchange (NYSE) and NASDAQ (the National Association of Securities Dealers Automated Quotation system). To buy stocks, you place an order with a broker. A broker is someone who carries out transactions between buyers and sellers. There are various types of brokers. Full-service brokerage companies, such as Merrill Lynch & Co., Inc., provide investment advice and recommendations along with processing transactions. Discount brokers, such as the Charles Schwab Corporation, place orders at a low price but provide only limited advice. Electronic brokers, such as E-Trade, allow you to place orders over the internet. In addition, some mutual fund companies offer brokerage services, allowing you to buy stocks as well as invest in mutual funds.

The Dow Jones Industrial Average tracks the health of thirty big companies in the United States during standard trading sessions.

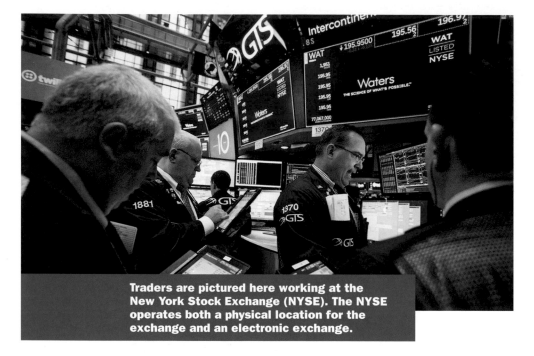

Traders are pictured here working at the New York Stock Exchange (NYSE). The NYSE operates both a physical location for the exchange and an electronic exchange.

Common and Preferred Stocks

There are two types of stock: common stock and preferred stock. Common stock is the type you are most likely to buy when starting out. There are two major differences between common and preferred stock. First, a company decides whether or not to pay a dividend (a percentage of the company's earnings paid to stockholders), and how much, to its common stockholders. The dividend may change from year to year, depending on how well the company is doing. Preferred stock pays a guaranteed dividend, but if a company does well and increases the dividend on the common stock, the preferred stock's dividend does not increase.

A second difference is what happens if a company fails. If a company goes out of business, the company's remaining assets are used to pay off bondholders and stockholders. However, bondholders are paid first, then preferred stockholders, and finally common stockholders. This procedure often means that when it's time to pay common stockholders, there is no money left, and so they lose their investment.

How Stocks Work

Stocks earn money in two ways. The first is by increasing in value. When a company's revenues (money it earns from sales) and profit are increasing, the value of a share of its stock increases, and people are willing to pay more for it. The difference between what you originally paid for a share of stock and its present value is called a capital gain (or capital loss, if its value goes down instead). Stocks may also pay dividends. The key to growing investments is reinvesting your capital gains and dividends. When you reinvest the money you make from investments, you buy more shares with it instead of spending it. Over time, you own more and more shares and have more and more gains and dividends.

When a company goes out of business, its remaining assets go first to bond- and stockholders.

Do I Need a Professional Adviser?

One question that most investors ask themselves at some point is whether or not they should handle their investments by themselves or use a professional broker. The following are some of the pros and cons of using a professional broker:

Pros

- The broker has more experience and is less likely to be influenced by the rumors and trends of the market.
- You may feel less nervous about your choices if you have someone knowledgeable to run your choices by.
- The broker may hear of new offerings you are not aware of.

Cons

- If you do not have a lot of money invested with the professional broker, you may not receive much attention.
- The broker may push you to purchase stocks that his or her company wants to sell or mutual funds on which he or she receives a commission (a percentage of the purchase price paid to the broker by the fund company).
- The broker may be more aggressive or conservative in his or her investing than you are comfortable with.

At one time, investors had only two choices: work with a full-service broker or invest on your own with no professional advice. This is no longer the case. Many discount and online brokerages, such as Charles Schwab, offer lower fees than full-service brokers but provide access to professionals who can advise you either free of charge or for an additional fee on an as-needed basis.

10 Great Questions to Ask a Financial Adviser

1. What combination of investments would you recommend for someone my age?

2. What stocks would you recommend for someone my age?

3. Is it OK for me to invest in Company X?

4. Where's the best place to put money I might need in a few years when I go to college?

5. How often should I check back with you about how my investments are doing?

6. Under what conditions should I consider selling some of my stocks?

7. Under what conditions should I consider buying more stocks?

8. What bank account or money market account is paying the best interest rate right now?

9. What CDs are paying the best interest rate right now?

10. What kinds of changes in my life should I let you know about so we can adjust my mix of investments?

CHAPTER FIVE

Investing Principles

All investments involve some type of risk. But if you follow a few basic principles, you can keep the risk at a level that is manageable.

Don't Put All Your Eggs in One Basket

The key to protecting the money you invest is diversification. If you have all your money in stocks, and the stock market goes down, your portfolio (collection of investments) will probably decline at a rate similar to that of the market as a whole. However, if two-thirds of your money is in stocks and one-third is in bonds, then your portfolio will most likely decline less than the stock market as a whole. Putting some of your money in stocks and some of your money in bonds is an example of diversification. As an investor, you can diversify even more by putting together a

Allocati...
alues listed below do not inc...
: & Allocation for

CASH EQUIVALENTS
PRINCIPAL PRESERVATION
BALANCED
LARGE CAP STOCKS
MID/SMALL CAP STOCKS
INTERNATIONAL STOCK
WORLD STOCK
SHORT TERM FIXED INCOME
LONG/INTERMEDIATE TERM FIXED
HIGH YIELD FIXED INCOME
INTERNATIONAL FIX...

$159,...
$3,937.91
$124,361.8
$34,629
$55,49

A pie chart like the one shown here can provide a helpful look—with one glance—at how your portfolio is diversified.

combination of different categories of investments, such as stocks, bonds, CDs, and cash. You will also need to select a variety of stocks and bonds within each category. Remember that your goal is to make as much money as possible, while still protecting the money you invest.

Industries and Categories

Experts divide stocks into general categories based on industry. These industrial categories are called sectors. Most experts recommend that a diversified portfolio should include five to ten stocks in different industries. For instance, health care, technology, retail, and energy are all different sectors. Why are sectors important? Because as various events affect the economy, companies in some sectors do well and others do worse. For example, when the economy is doing well and people's wages are going up, retail stores tend to do well. When the economy is doing poorly, companies that provide necessities like health care and food do well, but retail stores do poorly because people have less money to spend on items like clothing. It is important to make sure that the stocks you own are in different sectors because that way you will have some stocks that can do well, no matter what happens in the economy. This diversification helps protect you against large overall losses.

Sometimes, people see that one sector is hot, such as technology during the rise of the internet, or energy when the price of oil and gas increases. They are tempted to concentrate their investments in these sectors. However, sooner or later the prospects for those industries start to look less exciting. People and institutions that invested large sums of money in those sectors cash their money out, taking profits, and the stock prices tumble. At that point, you can lose large sums of money.

The construction of oil refineries like the one shown here affect the price of oil and gas.

Analyzing Stocks

How do you know if a stock is good to invest in? There are a number of standard measures you can use to evaluate a stock. There are a variety of printed and online sources that provide financial information on individual stocks. Online sources include free sources like Yahoo! Finance and fee-based research resources, such as Value Line (www.valueline.com). Although the format of information provided varies from source to source, when you input the ticker symbol (one or more letters that identify a stock on a stock exchange) for a stock in an online source or look it up in a printed resource, you will see information that looks similar to this:

Fabulous Company, Inc. (FCI)

Last Trade	121.73
Net Change	-2.85
Net Change %	-2.29%
Bid	121.63
Ask	122.29
Day High	123.99
Day Low	119.67
Volume	7,155.323
52-Week High	130.93 on 07/23/2009
52-Week Low	97.04 on 01/11/2009
P/E	15
EPS	8.15
Dividend & %	2.00 (1.60%)
Capitalization	16.90B

"Last Trade" is the most recent per share price that the stock was purchased at. "Net Change" is how much the stock has gone up or down in dollars and cents. "Net Change %" is how much the stock has gone up or down as a percentage. "Bid" is the most recent amount offered for the stock. "Ask" is the most recent amount someone has offered to sell the stock for. "Day High" and "Day Low" are the highest price and lowest price, respectively, that the stock has

By carefully analyzing individual stocks, you can decide whether or not they are worth investing in.

sold for that day. "Volume" is how many shares have been traded in the last day. "52-Week High" and "Low" show the highest and lowest price the stock has traded at in the past year. The next four items are the most commonly used in evaluating a stock.

When you are considering which stock to buy, you can't just look at the price of the stock. Since companies have different levels of earnings and the price reflects what investors think the earnings will be, a stock that sells for $10 and a stock that sells for $50 may both be fairly valued if the $50 stock has much greater earnings. Instead, investors use a measure called the price-to-earnings (P/E) ratio. To get the P/E ratio, you divide the price of one share of stock by the amount of earnings per share. For example, the price of a share of stock in Fabulous Company, Inc. is $121.75, and its earnings per share are $8.15, so:

$$121.75 \div 8.15 = 14.9, \text{ which is rounded up to } 15$$

Thus, FCI's P/E ratio is 15. Generally, the lower the number is, the better. For example, if two companies are equally promising,

Stock prices, like these from Amazon.com, are volatile, meaning that they rise and fall in response to many factors.

but one has a P/E of 10 and the other has a P/E of 15, the one that has a P/E of 10 is a better value (costs less per dollar of earnings).

Earnings per share (EPS) is the amount of earnings the company generates per each share of stock that exists. The more earnings per share a company generates, the better. A dividend is a percentage of profits that the company pays to stockholders. Dividend in dollars and percent (Dividend & %) shows the current dividend that the company pays per each share of stock and the percent of earnings that the dividend represents. Not all companies issue dividends; some fast-growing companies reinvest their profits in the company to fuel their growth instead. However, among companies that do pay dividends, this measure will give you an idea of how much the company pays out to shareholders, compared to other companies.

Market capitalization is the total number of outstanding shares times the price per share. Companies are divided into large cap (greater than $5 billion), midcap ($1 to $5 billion), and small cap stocks (under $1 billion). Generally, the smaller the market cap of a stock, the riskier it is.

Many company listings provide additional information as well. This information should include several years of financial information. Examining this information will allow you to see if the company is financially sound and if its revenues and earnings have been increasing on a regular basis. From the financials, you can see how fast a company is growing. The stock of a company that grows in revenues and earnings faster than similar companies has a good chance of outperforming their stock. One important element is how much debt (loans) the company has. In general, less debt is better than a lot of debt. If business conditions take a downturn, companies with a lot of debt may have trouble repaying it. In addition, the report may include information on the company's business activities, its position in comparison to its competitors, and prospects for the sector that the company is part of. All this information is important in making a judgment about whether or not the stock is a good investment.

Learning About Technical Analysis

Technical analysis refers to the use of standard mathematical formulas and charts to evaluate stocks and sectors. In recent years, some brokers have developed a series of mathematical measures that track various elements of stock performance. These measures are based on theories proposed by some economists, stating that when the chart of a stock's performance conforms to certain patterns, the stock's value will go up or down. Although referring to such charts can be useful for supplementing fundamental analysis, relying on technical analysis alone can be dangerous.

The Unpredictable Market

No matter how well you analyze the stock market, how many investment books you read, or how many charts you study, the ultimate behavior of stocks is never totally predictable. Unexpected events can easily cause the market to go up or down. The terrorist attacks of 9/11, the fall of the Berlin Wall, and the end of communism in Russia were all unpredictable.

The best way to protect your money, given the basic unpredictability of the market, is to buy low and sell high. The reason for this, as explained by Nassim Nicholas Taleb in his book *The Black Swan*, is that if you buy stock that is expensive and it goes down, you can lose a lot of money. Also, if you pay a lot for it, it may not go up much more. Thus, you stand to lose a lot of money if something bad happens but not gain that much if it doesn't. In contrast, if you buy a stock that's cheap, you can't lose too much money per share if it goes down because it can only go to zero. But if your analysis is correct and it is a good company, it could potentially go up a lot and you can make money.

What does "buying low" mean? It does not mean buying stocks that cost only a few dollars. It means that you should buy stocks that are cheap in relation to their potential earnings. It means that you should buy a stock whose price is lower than you think it should be, given that the company is fundamentally sound and you think its earnings will continue to do well. Similarly, the best time to sell stocks is when they have gone up a lot. This is especially true if you are young. The market will not stay up—or down—forever. You will see many economic cycles in your lifetime. Your job is to take advantage of these cyclical changes by buying good stocks when they are cheap. Keep in mind that it's always best to buy and sell stock in increments because you have no way of knowing whether or not a stock is going to go up or down more. For example, if you want to buy one hundred shares of stock, it's safest to buy it twenty-five shares at a time, so that you can take advantage of it going up or down further.

Clubs for Investing

One excellent way to learn about investing firsthand is through an investment club. Many high schools and colleges sponsor such clubs. A teacher supervises the club. In high school clubs, students can invest either real or virtual (make-believe) money. If students use real money, the signed permission of parents or guardians is required to participate, and an adult must place the actual orders to buy and sell the stock because the students are minors. Either way, the students themselves choose the companies to

An investment club can be a fun way to learn about money matters while building friendships at the same time.

invest in, perform research on the companies, track their stocks' performance, and make any other investment decisions.

How the Economy Affects Investments

The "economy" refers to the overall economic activity of a country. The state of the economy is measured by tracking the gross national product (GNP), the entire amount of income from all products and services provided in a year. The state of the economy affects the performance of stocks. When the GNP is growing, this means that people and companies are buying products and services in greater quantities than before. Therefore, companies are earning more. The prospect of increasing earnings tends to make the value of stocks go up.

Many things can affect the economy. One example is employment. The higher the unemployment rate, the fewer people who are working and have money to buy products and services; the reverse is true when unemployment is low. Another aspect is the availability of credit. Many businesses depend on being able to borrow money from banks to expand their businesses. When interest rates are low and credit is easily available, businesses can expand more easily and this expansion can lead to increased sales and profits.

Monitoring Your Investments

Regardless of how you keep track of your investments, it is important to review them on a regular basis. You want to evaluate each investment not only to see if it is gaining or losing money but also to consider if anything basic has changed about the company you are invested in. Some people review investments weekly or monthly. It is a good idea to review your investments at least a couple of times per year.

Myths and Facts

Myth: The best way to save for a special occasion is to have the bank deduct money automatically once each month from your account and place it in a Christmas club or other special account.

Fact: The interest rate on such accounts is often lower than on a regular savings account. So it might be better to open a regular savings account (separate from any others you have) for that purpose and make monthly deposits yourself.

Myth: If a stock or sector keeps going up, it is hot and I should invest in it.

Fact: Investing lots of money in hot sectors can cost you money because (1) by the time you are aware that the sector is hot, it's already had most of its gains, and (2) large investors who are all following the same trend are likely to decide to pull their money out at the same time, causing a rapid drop in those stocks.

Myth: Professional brokers have inside information I don't have.

Fact: Laws passed in recent years have made it illegal for corporate officers to tell brokers information that they don't share with the general public. So all the relevant news about a company is available if you take the time to look for it.

GLOSSARY

ask The price that someone is offering to sell a stock at.

balance The amount of money currently in an account.

bid The price that someone is offering to buy a stock for.

bouncing a check Having a check presented to your bank that you don't have enough money in your account to pay.

broker A person who performs transactions between buyers and sellers.

capital gain (loss) The amount of increase (or decrease) in the value of shares of stock.

commission A percentage of the sale price of an item paid to the person who sells it.

deduct To subtract from an account.

deferred Put off until a future date.

deposit To put money into.

diversified Including many different types.

dividend A share of profits paid by a company to its shareholders.

Dow Jones Industrial Average An index consisting of thirty industrial companies whose stocks' performances provide a standard measure of the stock market's value.

economic cycle A series of changes in the overall business activities in a country that occurs over and over.

exchange A company that provides facilities to trade stocks, bonds, mutual funds, or other types of investments.

increment One of a series of regular additions or contributions.

index A group of companies whose stock represents the typical performance of a market or sector.

individual retirement account (IRA) A type of investment account that provides tax advantages to encourage people to save for retirement.

interest An amount paid for the use of money.

interest rate The percentage of a sum of money paid for its use.

junk bond A bond issued by a high-risk company. Such bonds pay a high interest rate but carry an above-average danger that the company might fail.

personal identification number (PIN) A series of numbers used to verify your identity.

portfolio A collection of investments.

principal The sum of money you put into an investment.

reconcile To make sure that your financial records agree with the bank's and are accurate.

return on investment The amount of money you make from an investment, in dollars or as a percentage.

withdrawal The money you remove from an account.

FOR MORE INFORMATION

Canadian Bankers Association (CBA)
Box 348
Commerce Court West
199 Bay Street, 30th Floor
Toronto, ON M5L 1G2
Canada
(800) 263-0231
Email: inform@cba.ca
Website: http://www.cba.ca
Twitter: @CdnBankers
The Canadian Bankers Association provides information
   about budgeting, credit, investments, and banking
   in Canada.

Federal Deposit Insurance Corporation (FDIC)
Consumer Response Center
1100 Walnut Street, Box #11
Kansas City, MO 64106
(877) 275-3342
Website: http://www.fdic.gov
Facebook and Twitter: @FDICgov
The FDIC insures bank accounts in the United States.
   The FDIC's website provides a variety of information
   related to banking and the state of banks.

Fidelity Investments
PO Box 770001

Cincinnati, OH 45277
(800) 972-2155
Website: http://www.fidelity.com
Facebook: @fidelityinvestments
Twitter: @fidelity
The number-one US provider of retirement accounts, this
    company provides information on retirement and
    nonretirement investing. Its website provides the
    latest news and real-time quotes.

House Financial Services Committee
2129 Rayburn House Office Building
Washington, DC 20515
(202) 225-7502
Website: http://financialservices.house.gov
Facebook and Twitter: @FinancialCmte
This committee is responsible for dealing with financial
    issues and bills. It is possible to view hearings over
    the internet and obtain information on various bills
    that have been passed and are under consideration
    and their potential effects on the economy.

Investment Industry Regulatory Organization of Canada
121 King Street West, Suite 2000
Toronto, ON M5H 3T9
Canada
(416) 364-6133
Website: http://www.iiroc.ca
Facebook: @iiroc
Twitter: @iirocinfo

This is the organization that regulates stock transactions
in Canada and provides information about
stock rules.

New York Stock Exchange
11 Wall Street
New York, NY 10005
(212) 896-2830
Website: http://www.nyse.com
Facebook, Twitter, and Instagram: @nyse
This is the best-known stock exchange in the United
States. Its website provides a variety of information
related to stocks.

Securities Investment Protection Corporation
1667 K Street NW, Suite 1000
Washington, DC 20006-1620 (202) 371-8300
Website: http://www.sipc.org/contact.cfm
Facebook: @sipcorg
Twitter: @sipc
This organization insures investment accounts. It
also provides information on protections for
investment accounts.

US Department of the Treasury
1500 Pennsylvania Avenue SW
Washington, DC 20220
(202) 622-2000
Website: http://home.treasury.gov
Facebook and Twitter: @ustreasury
The Treasury Department monitors and manages the
overall state of the US economy. Its website includes

the latest information on financial markets, as well as information on the various types of bonds issued by the federal government.

US Securities and Exchange Commission
100 F Street NE
Washington, DC 20549
(202) 942-8080
Website: http://www.sec.gov
Facebook: @SECInvestorEducation
Twitter: @SEC_Investor_ed
This is the organization that regulates investing in the United States. It provides educational written publications and a variety of useful calculators on its website.

Vanguard
PO Box 2600
Valley Forge, PA 19482
(877) 662-7447
Website: http://www.vanguard.com
Facebook: @vanguard
Twitter: @vanguard_group
This is the company that pioneered the index mutual fund, which contains the same companies found in major indexes. Its website provides market news.

FOR FURTHER READING

Bickerstaff, Linda. *Smart Strategies for Saving and Building Wealth*. New York, NY: Rosen Publishing, 2015.

Hardyman, Robyn. *Understanding Income and Savings*. New York, NY: Rosen Publishing, 2018.

Hardyman, Robyn. *Understanding Money Goals and Budgeting*. New York, NY: Rosen Publishing, 2018.

Hardyman, Robyn. *Understanding Stocks and Investing*. New York, NY: Rosen Publishing, 2018.

Marsico, Katie. *Using Credit Wisely*. Ann Arbor, MI: Cherry Lake Publishing, 2016.

McGuire, Kara. *Making Money Work: The Teens' Guide To Saving, Investing, and Building Wealth*. North Mankato, MN: Capstone Young Readers, 2015.

McGuire, Kara. *The Teen Money Manual: A Guide to Cash, Credit, Spending, Saving, Work, Wealth, and More*. North Mankato, MN: Capstone Young Readers, 2015.

Minden, Cecelia. *Living on a Budget*. Ann Arbor, MI: Cherry Lake Publishing, 2016.

Nagle, Jeanne. *Money, Banking, and Finance*. New York, NY: Rosen Publishing, 2018.

Peterson, Judy Monroe. *Smart Strategies for Investing Wisely and Successfully*. New York, NY: Rosen Publishing, 2015.

Schlesinger, Emily, and Jennifer Liss. *Managing Money*. Costa Mesa, CA: Saddleback Educational Publishing, 2017.

Weeks, Marcus, and Derek Braddon. *Heads Up Money*. New York, NY: DK Publishing, 2016.

BIBLIOGRAPHY

Bahney, Anna. "40% of Americans Can't Cover a $400 Emergency Expense." CNN Money. https://money.cnn.com/2018/05/22/pf/emergency-expenses-household-finances/index.html.

Cramer, Jim. *Real Money: Sane Investing in an Insane World*. New York, NY: Simon & Schuster, 2005.

Elmblad, Shelley. "Pros and Cons of the Mint App." The Balance, October 7, 2018. http://www.thebalance.com/mint-com-manages-accounts-budgets-and-more-online-1293882.

IRS. "IRA FAQs." https://www.irs.gov/retirement-plans/retirement-plans-faqs-regarding-iras.

IRS. "Retirement Topics - IRA Contribution Limits." Retirement Topics IRA Contribution Limits. October 20, 2017. http://www.irs.gov/retirement-plans/plan-participant-employee/retirement-topics-ira-contribution-limits.

Kansas, Dave. *The Wall Street Journal Complete Guide to Money and Investing*. New York, NY: Three Rivers Press, 2005.

Money. "How to Make the Best of a Bad Situation." September 2008, pp. 78–84.

Money. "When to Start Saving for Retirement." http://time.com/money/collection-post/4138306/save-for-retirement-young.

Morris, Virginia B., and Kenneth Morris. *Standard & Poor's Guide to Money and Investing.* New York, NY: McGraw-Hill, 2005.

Taleb, Nassim Nicholas. *The Black Swan: The Impact of the Highly Improbable.* New York, NY: Random House, 2007.

US Securities and Exchange Commission. "Protect Your Money: Check Out Brokers and Investment Advisors." January 24, 2012. https://www.sec.gov/reportspubs/investor -publications/investor -brokershtm.html.

INDEX

ABOUT THE AUTHORS

Xina M. Uhl has authored a variety of books for young people in addition to textbooks, teacher's guides, lessons, and assessment questions. She has a BA from Arizona State University and an MA from California State University Northridge. When she is not writing or reading, she enjoys travel, photography, and hiking with her dogs. Her blog features her travel adventures and latest fiction projects.

Jeri Freedman has a BA degree from Harvard University. For fifteen years, she worked for high-technology companies, where her duties included investor relations. She has been an active investor for twenty-five years.

PHOTO CREDITS